☺ Early Learning

Sticker Activity

ABC

priddy ☺ books

big ideas for little people

A a

Apple, ax and astronaut -
what other words
begin with "a"?

apple

ax

ant

astronaut

Where would you
travel to if you were
an astronaut?

B b

What insect flies and goes
"buzz, buzz"? Can you find
something else that flies?

baby

butterfly

What other "b"
words do you see?

bumblebee

bulldozer

C c

What do you think
each of these objects
feels like?

coconut

Which of these turns
into a butterfly?

cactus

caterpillar

cat

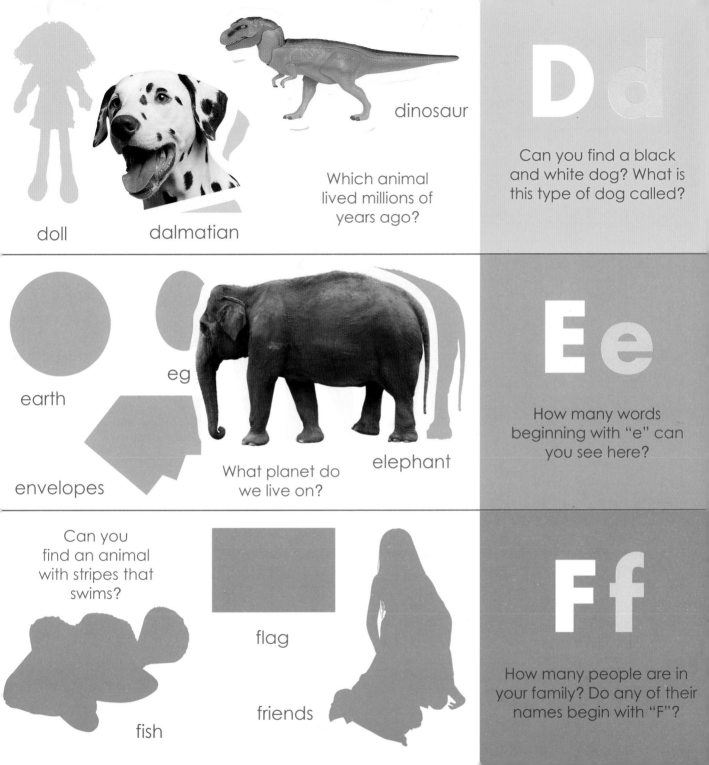

doll

dalmatian

dinosaur

Which animal lived millions of years ago?

D d

Can you find a black and white dog? What is this type of dog called?

earth

eg

envelopes

elephant

What planet do we live on?

E e

How many words beginning with "e" can you see here?

Can you find an animal with stripes that swims?

flag

friends

fish

F f

How many people are in your family? Do any of their names begin with "F"?

G g

Which "g" is juicy, sweet and delicious to eat?

goat

grapes

girl

Who's making a silly face - the goat or the girl?

H h

How many windows does this house have?

What "h" has five fingers?

house

hand

I i

Which "i" is hot and which "i" is cold?

iron

ice cream

Don't ever touch a hot iron!

iguana

J j

Which of these things can't you eat?

What can you put on your toast that begins with "j"?

juice

jelly

jeans

K k

What do you use to open your front door?

kettle

keys

koala

Can you find two shiny objects that begin with "k"?

L l

lizard

ladybugs

Which fruits taste sour?

lemon

lime

Does a lizard prefer to eat lemons or ladybugs?

M m

Can you think of any other "m" words?

motorcycle

How many "m"s are in the word "mommy"?

N n

Do you know which number comes next?

1 2 3 4
5 6 7 8

numbers

How old are you? Is your age one of these numbers?

O o

What noise does an owl make?

Which vegetable makes your eyes water?

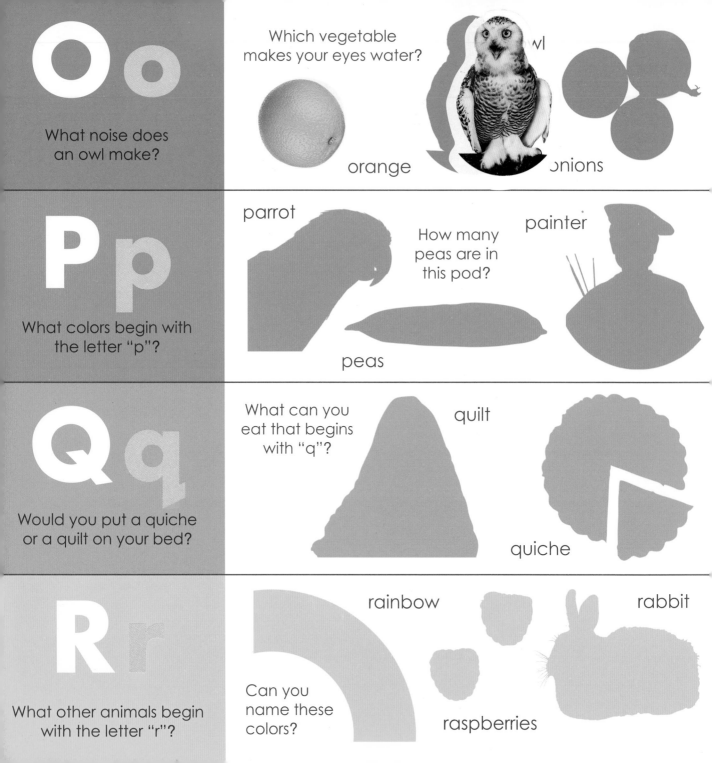

orange

owl

onions

P p

What colors begin with the letter "p"?

parrot

How many peas are in this pod?

painter

peas

Q q

Would you put a quiche or a quilt on your bed?

What can you eat that begins with "q"?

quilt

quiche

R r

What other animals begin with the letter "r"?

rainbow

rabbit

Can you name these colors?

raspberries

spade

seagull

starfish

How many of these are found at the beach?

spider

S s

What other "s" words can you find by the sea?

toucan

truck

What other things that go begin with "t"?

T t

What "t" do you show when you smile?

When would you use an umbrella?

undress

under

umbrella

U u

What's the opposite of "down"?

What vegetables do you like to eat?

vegetables

V v

What letters do these vegetables begin with?

W w

What would you put in a watering can?

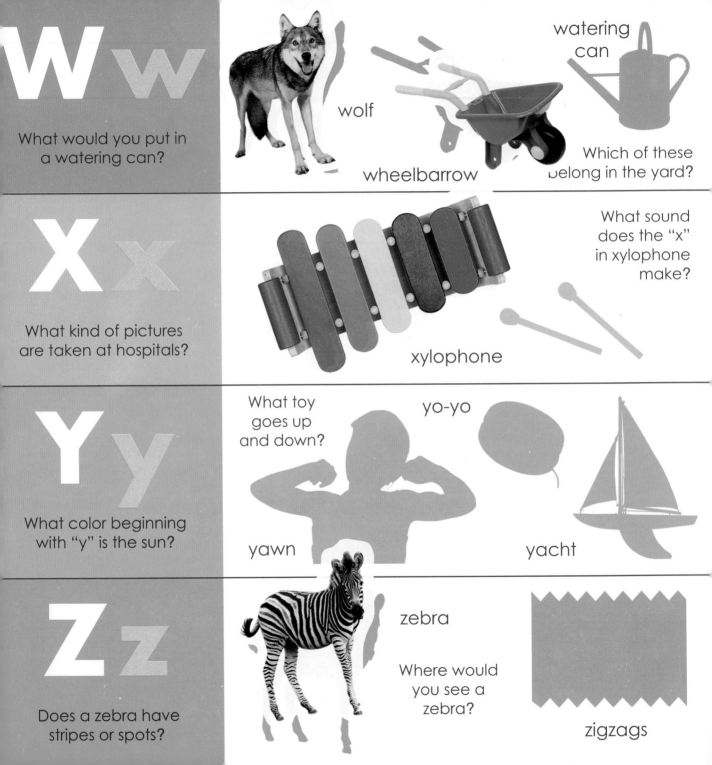

wolf

wheelbarrow

watering can

Which of these belong in the yard?

X x

What kind of pictures are taken at hospitals?

What sound does the "x" in xylophone make?

xylophone

Y y

What color beginning with "y" is the sun?

What toy goes up and down?

yo-yo

yawn

yacht

Z z

Does a zebra have stripes or spots?

zebra

Where would you see a zebra?

zigzags

See if you can find out where these letter stickers belong.

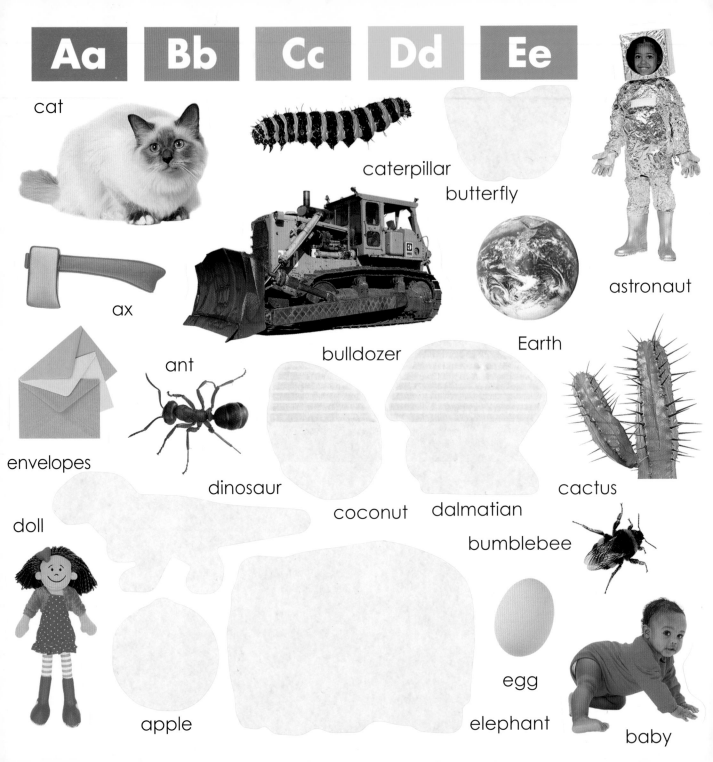

Aa **Bb** **Cc** **Dd** **Ee**

cat

caterpillar

butterfly

astronaut

ax

Earth

bulldozer

envelopes

ant

cactus

dinosaur

coconut dalmatian

cactus

doll

bumblebee

egg

apple elephant

baby

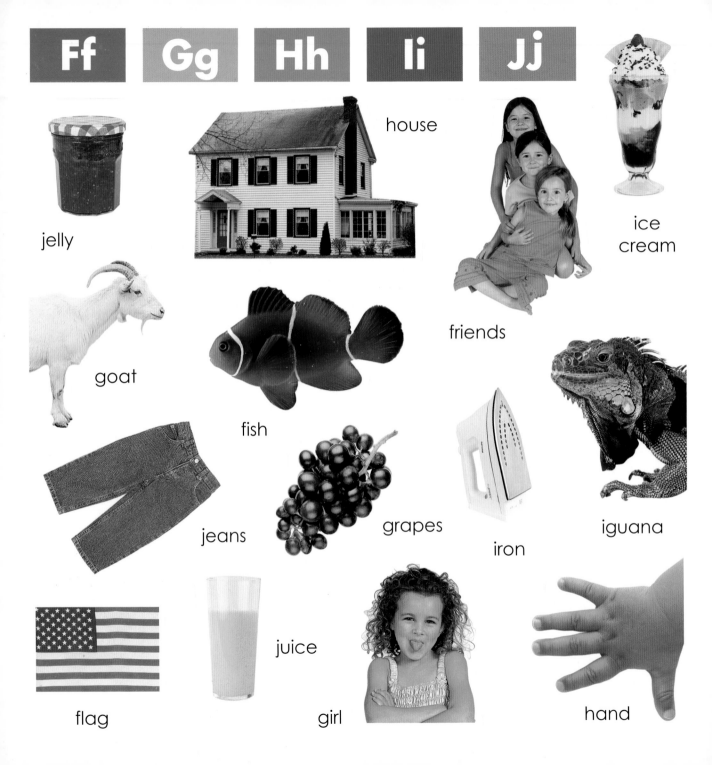

Ff Gg Hh Ii Jj

jelly

house

ice cream

friends

goat

fish

iguana

jeans

grapes

iron

flag

juice

girl

hand

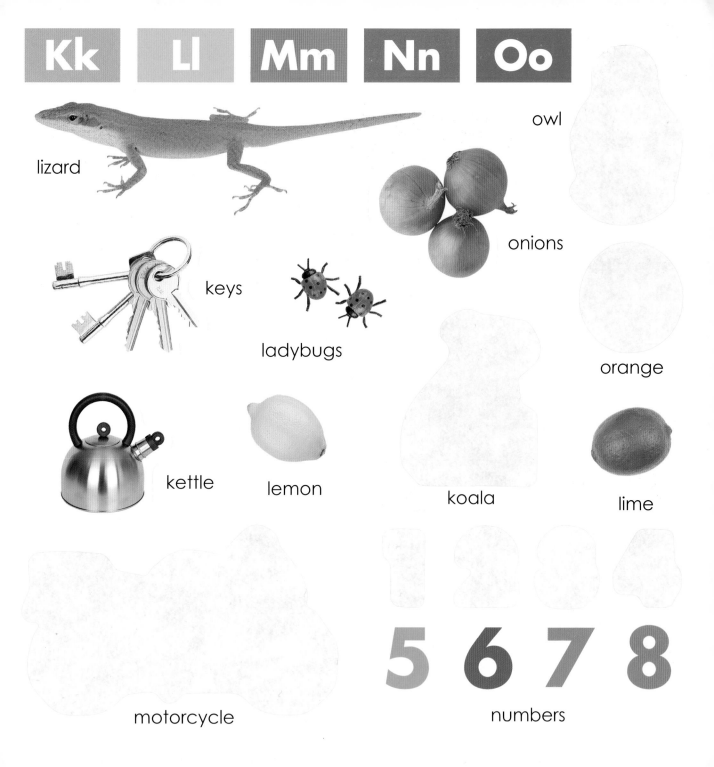

Kk Ll Mm Nn Oo

lizard

owl

keys

onions

ladybugs

orange

kettle

lemon

koala

lime

motorcycle

5 6 7 8

numbers

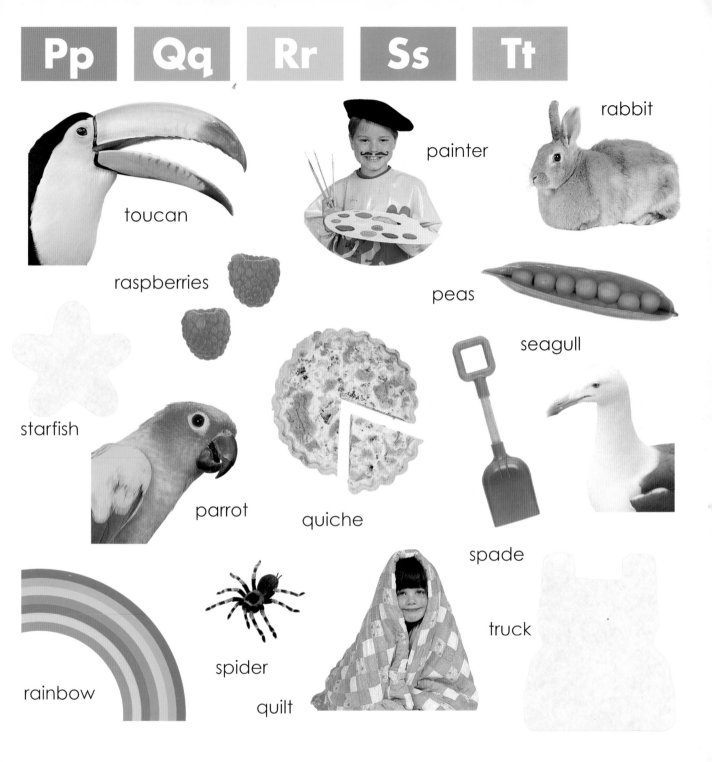

Pp **Qq** **Rr** **Ss** **Tt**

toucan

painter

rabbit

raspberries

peas

seagull

starfish

parrot

quiche

spade

rainbow

spider

quilt

truck

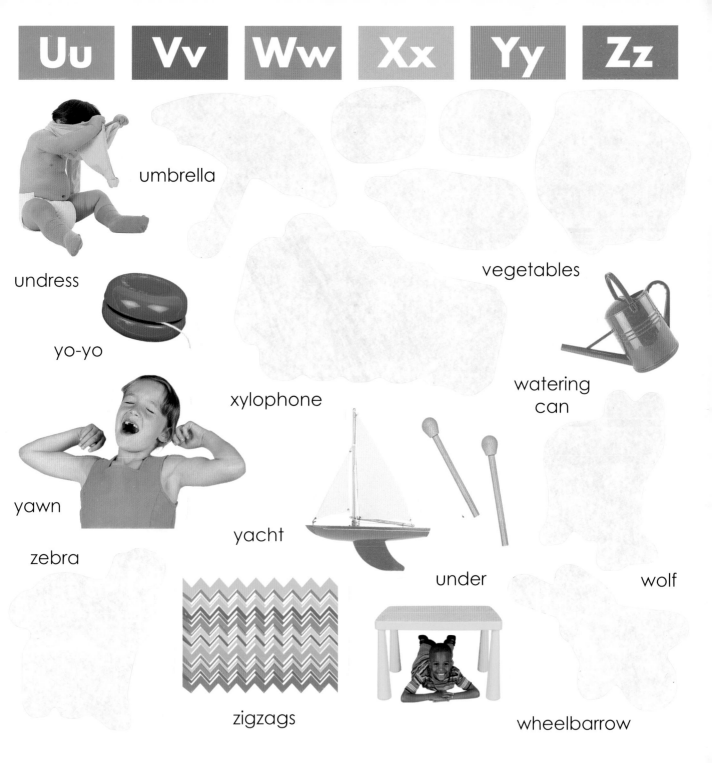

Uu Vv Ww Xx Yy Zz

umbrella

undress

yo-yo

xylophone

vegetables

watering can

yawn

yacht

zebra

under

wolf

zigzags

wheelbarrow

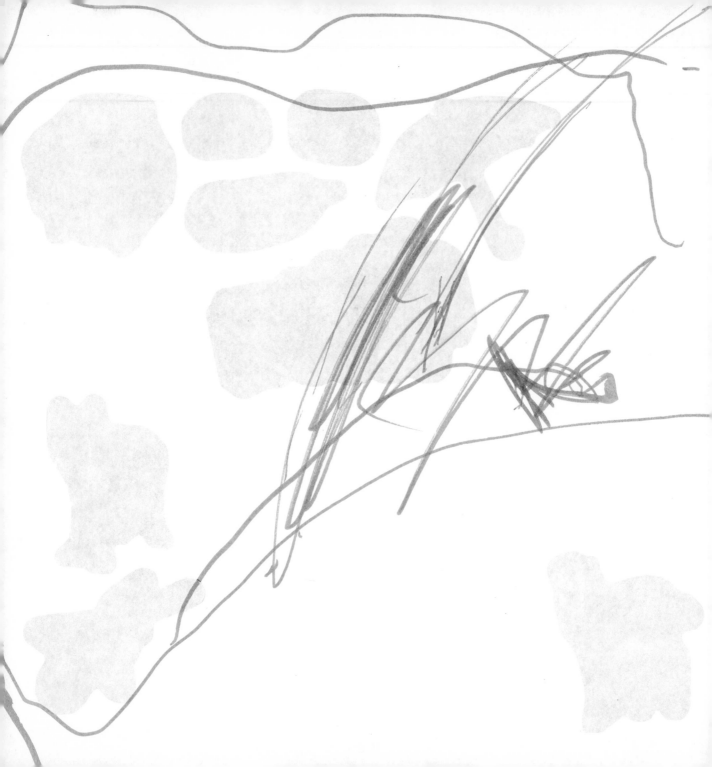

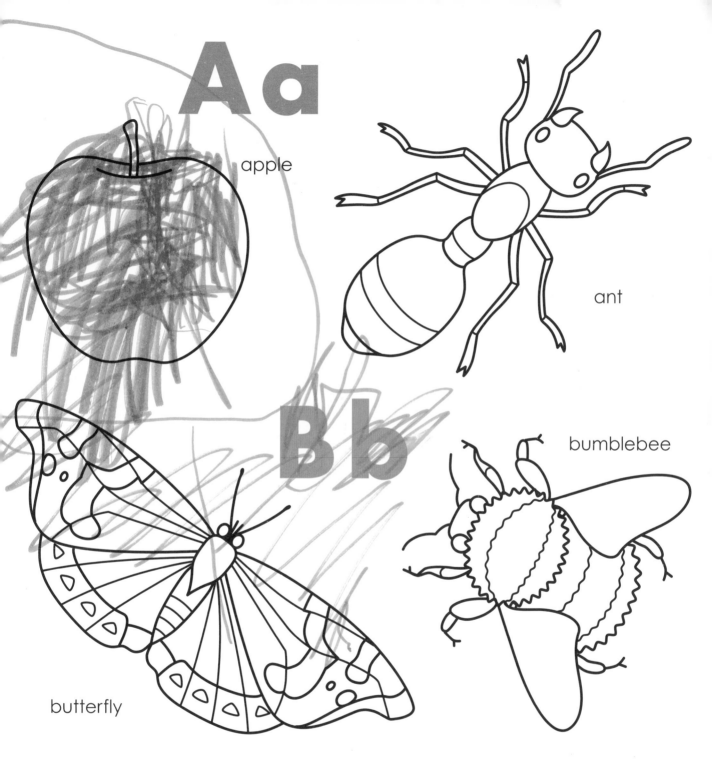

Aa

apple

ant

Bb

bumblebee

butterfly

Cc

cat

chicken

Dd

drum

dinosaur

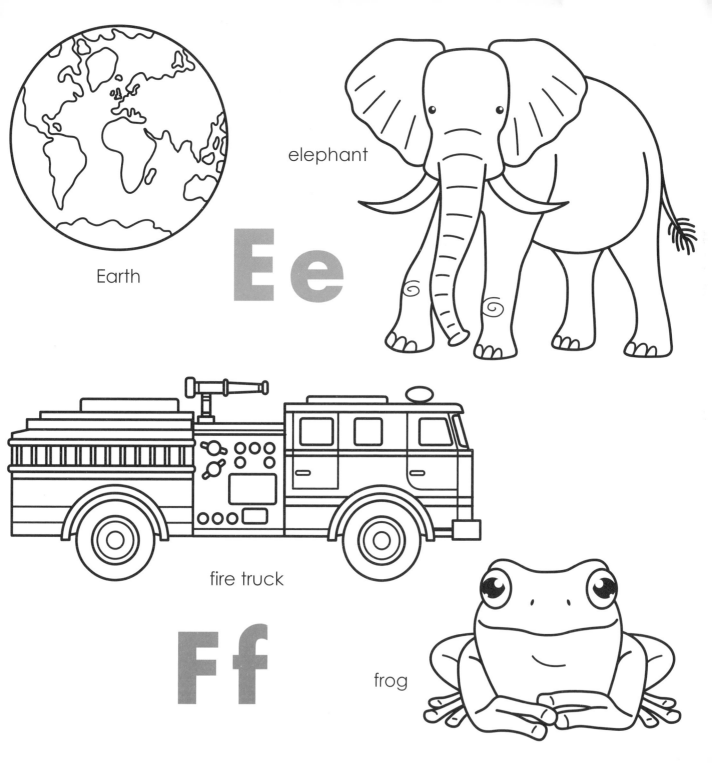

Earth

Ee

elephant

fire truck

Ff

frog

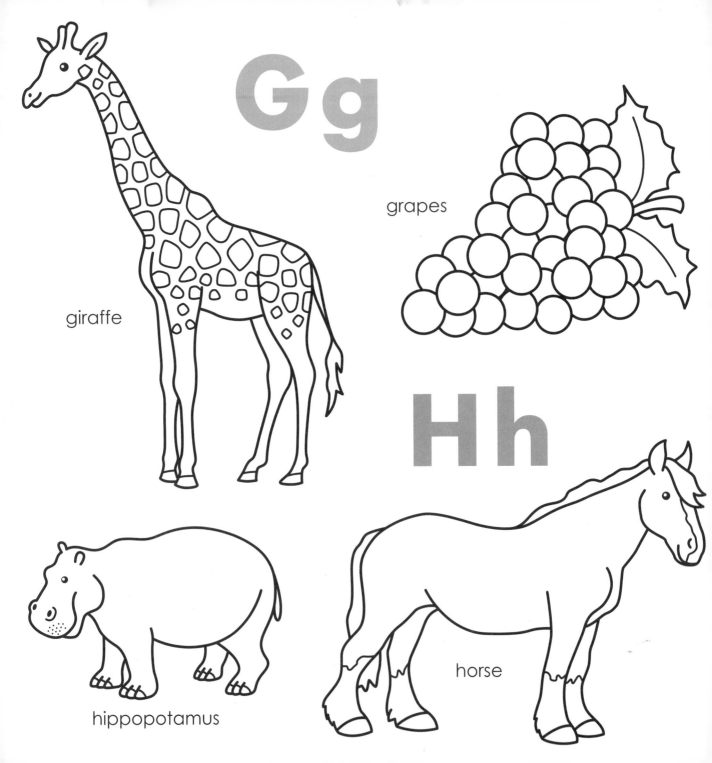

G g

giraffe

grapes

H h

hippopotamus

horse

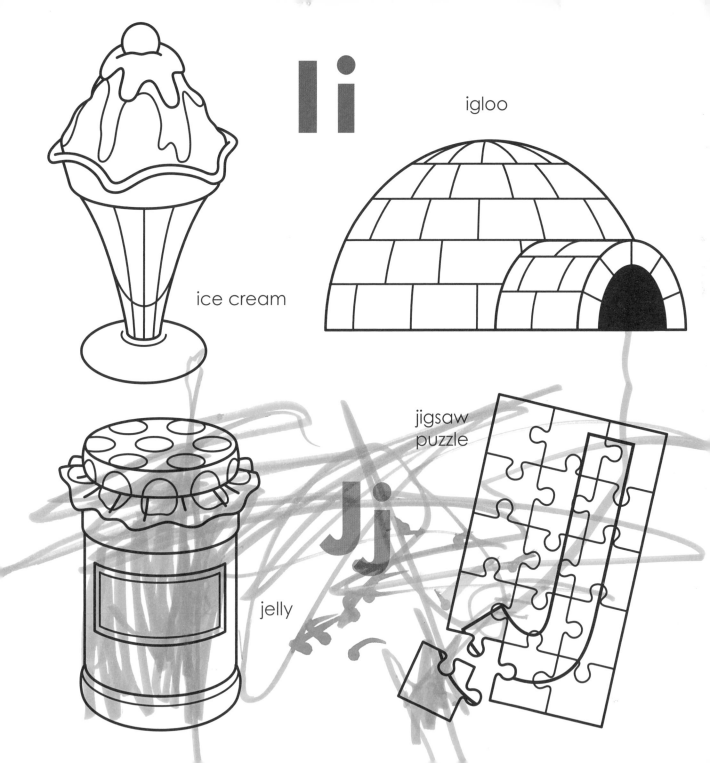

Ii

ice cream

igloo

Jj

jelly

jigsaw puzzle

Kk

kettle

koala

Ll

ladybug

lemon

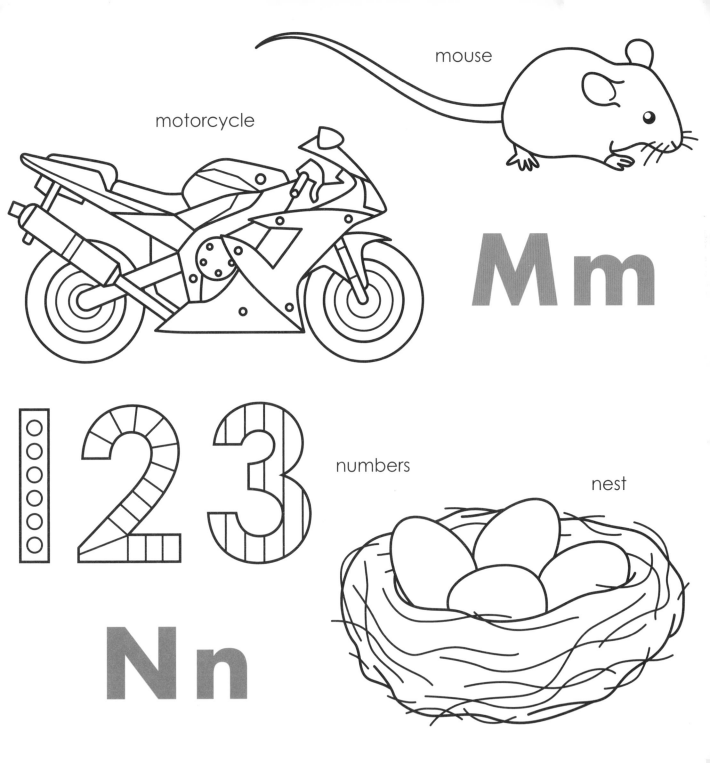

mouse

motorcycle

Mm

numbers

nest

Nn

Oo

owl

Pp

penguin

pencils

Qq

queen

Rr

rainbow

rabbit

Ss

sunflower

sandwich

T t

train

tiger

umbrella

U u

unicycle

Vv

violin

vegetables

Ww

watering can

wolf

X x

xylophone

yo-yo

Y y

yacht

zebra

Z z

zigzag

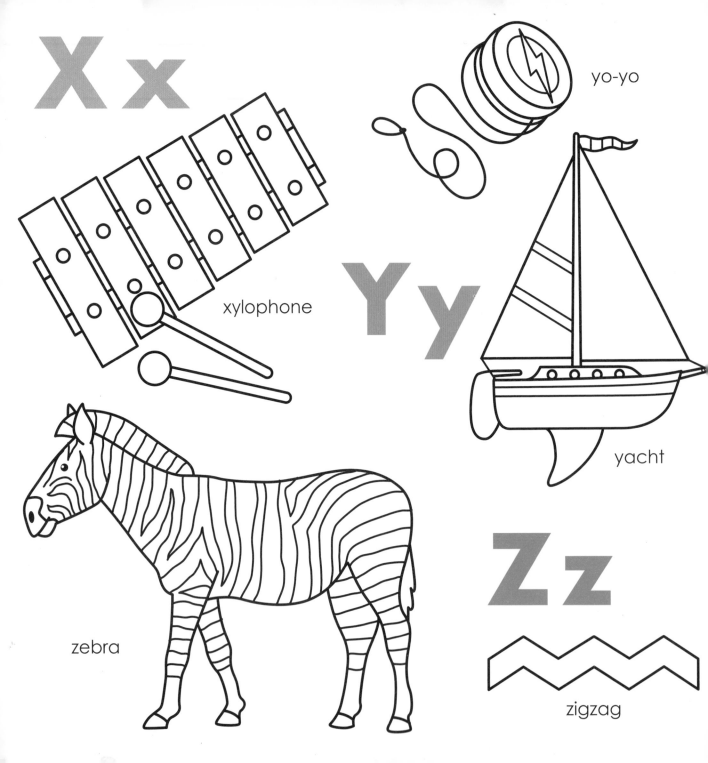